WHO, WHAT, WHY?

WHO WERE
THE DISCIPLES?

DANIKA COOLEY

T0419606

CF4KIDS

10 9 8 7 6 5 4 3 2 1
Copyright © Danika Cooley 2025
Paperback 978-1-5271-1279-7
ebook ISBN: 978-1-5271-1336-7

Published by
Christian Focus Publications,
Geanies House, Fearn, Tain, Ross-shire,
IV20 1TW, Scotland, U.K.
www.christianfocus.com
email: info@christianfocus.com

Printed and bound by Bell and Bain, Glasgow

Cover design by Catriona Mackenzie
Illustrations by Martyn Smith

TABLE OF CONTENTS

Chapter One: Calling the Fishers of Men 7

Chapter Two: Simon Peter, the Rock 13

Chapter Three: Andrew, the Bringer of People 19

Chapter Four: James, the Son of Thunder 25

Chapter Five: John, the Beloved Disciple 31

Chapter Six: Philip, the Slow of Heart 38

Chapter Seven: Nathanael Bartholomew,
  the True of Heart 44

Chapter Eight: Matthew Levi, the Tax Collector 50

Chapter Nine: Thomas, the Twin 56

Chapter Ten: James, the Younger 62

Chapter Eleven: Judas Lebbaeus Thaddaeus,
  not Iscariot...68

Chapter Twelve: Simon, the Zealot 75

Chapter Thirteen: Judas Iscariot, the Betrayer........ 81

Timeline 90

Works Consulted..94

Dedication

To the Reader (That's you!)
May you follow Jesus and tell others
about God's good news.

THE AUTHOR

Danika Cooley and her husband, Ed, are committed to leading their children to live for the glory of God. Danika has a passion for equipping parents to teach the Bible and Christian history to their kids. She is the author of *Help Your Kids Learn and Love the Bible*; *When Lightning Struck!: The Story of Martin Luther*; *Bible Investigators: Creation*; *Wonderfully Made: God's Story of Life from Conception to Birth*, and the *Who, What, Why?* series about the history of our faith. Danika's three year Bible survey curriculum, Bible Road Trip™, is used by families around the world. Weekly, she encourages tens of thousands of parents to intentionally raise biblically literate children. Danika is a homeschool mother of four with a Bachelor of Arts degree from the University of Washington. Find her at ThinkingKidsBlog.org.

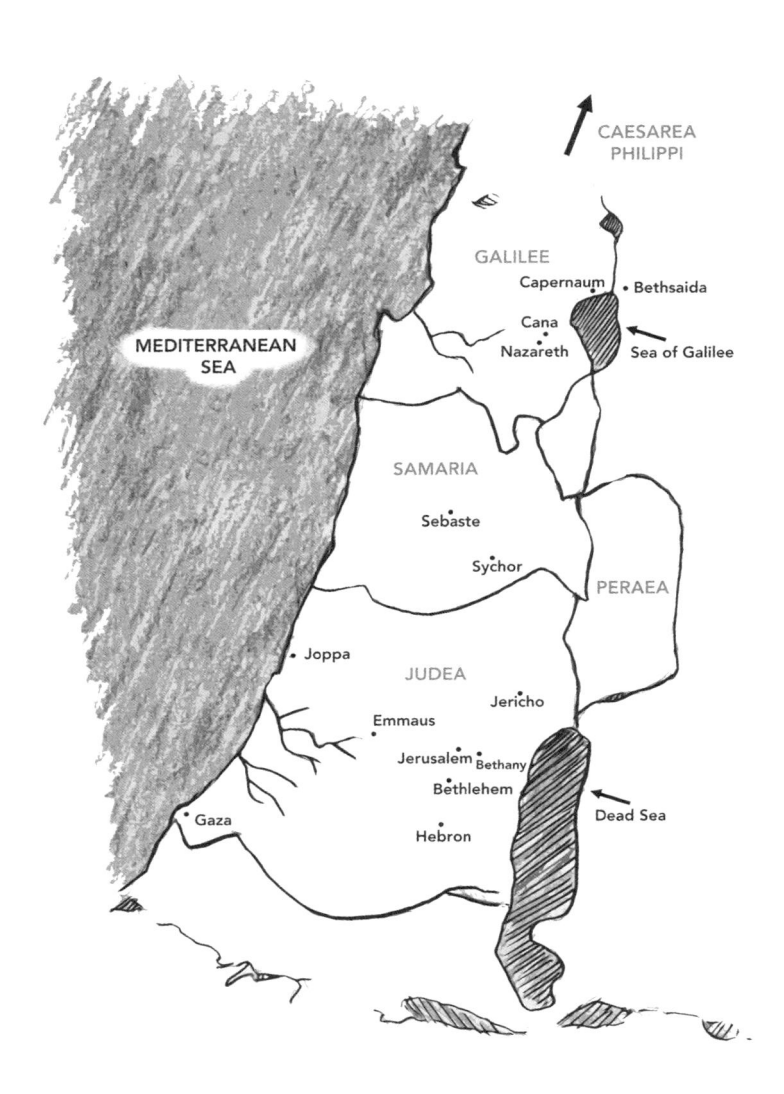

CALLING THE
FISHERS OF MEN

Have you ever felt as if there is nothing exciting God can do with your ho-hum, ordinary life? Throughout history, God has often chosen the most ho-hum, ordinary lives with which to do the most extraordinary things. God's marvelous work in history, you see, does not depend upon the amazingness of the people he chooses to work through. Rather, God's astonishing work in history is all about how incredible he is.

The most spectacular event in the whole of history was the work that Jesus did on the Cross. Now, Jesus is God the Son. For God is three Persons in one God: God the Father, God the Son, and God the Holy Spirit. When Jesus—who has always been God the Son—was born on earth to his mother Mary, it was a miracle. Inside the womb of a young Jewish woman, Jesus became both fully God and fully human—the Son of God, our Savior.

During his roughly three-year ministry, Jesus was followed by people everywhere he went. Some people who heard Jesus speak were interested only in the miracles he did, while others hoped he would lead a violent revolution to free Israel from the rule of the Roman Empire. The Bible often calls the many sincere followers of Jesus his disciples. Yet, Jesus chose just twelve ho-hum, ordinary men to be his special disciples, whom the Bible often refers to as the "Twelve."

One day, near the beginning of Jesus' ministry, he was teaching God's Word as he stood on the shore of the Sea of Galilee, a great big lake right in the middle of the land of the Jewish people. At that time, the former land of Israel was ruled by the Roman Empire, and divided into small regions, each with its own regional

ruler. For instance, Galilee, Judea, and Samaria were each their own region.

As Jesus spoke from the shore of the Sea of Galilee, scores of people were crowding to hear him, pushing Jesus slowly toward the water. Maybe his feet were even wet. Looking around, Jesus saw fishermen from two boats rinsing out their nets. Then Jesus, who is the King of Everything—the fish, the sea, the weather, and even fishermen—climbed into the boat of a man named Peter.

Jesus told Peter to take the boat out a little way from the shore. Sitting down, he taught the people

from the boat. When he finished teaching, Jesus said to Peter, "Put out into the deep and let down your nets for a catch (Luke 5:4)." Now, fishing is not easy. You can't just call the fish to jump into your nets. "We fished all night, Jesus, and we didn't catch anything," Peter said. "But, since it is you, I will let down the nets." So, Peter, and probably his brother, Andrew, threw the nets over the side.

Nothing with Jesus is ordinary, and he is King of Everything, so we should not be surprised that the nets began to fill with fish. There were so many fish that Peter and Andrew's nets began to tear under the strain. The brothers jumped up and down, calling for their business partners in the other boat to come and help them. James and John, the sons of Zebedee, quickly threw their nets over the side and hauled the flopping fish into their boat, too.

Once both boats were sinking under the weight of all the fish, Peter fell down in front of Jesus, right there among the flopping, slippery fish. "Leave me, Lord Jesus," he cried. "For I am a sinful man." Peter knew that not only was he an ordinary, ho-hum man, he was a sinner, as well. Peter also knew that Jesus is the perfect Son of God.

Jesus said, "Do not be afraid. From now on, you will be catching men (Luke 5:11)." That was the day that Peter, his brother Andrew, and the brothers James and John, left their boats and followed Jesus. They were going to be fishers of men—finders of men and women who will believe in and follow Jesus. They would be anything but ho-hum and ordinary.

WHAT IS A DISCIPLE?

Jesus' disciples learn from his teachings and obey his commands. They believe Jesus died on the Cross to take the punishment for our disobedience against God, called sin. Disciples repent—that means they turn away from sin and follow Jesus instead.

After Jesus died on the Cross and rose from the dead, he said, "Go therefore and make disciples of all nations, baptizing them in the name of the Father and of the Son and of the Holy Spirit, teaching them to observe all that I have commanded you. And behold, I am with you always, to the end of the age" (Matthew 28:19-20). A fisher of men doesn't just follow Jesus— he brings others to follow Jesus, too.

SIMON PETER,
THE ROCK

When Simon's brother Andrew first brought him to meet Jesus, Jesus immediately called him Peter, which means rock. Simon Peter was the son of a man named Jonah, from the region of Galilee in the northern part of Israel. Peter and Andrew were born in Bethsaida, but later moved six miles to Capernaum, where they ran a fishing business with another set of brothers, James and John.

Do you have a friend who says whatever comes to their mind? That's what Peter was like. Out of all the disciples, he asked the most questions, he answered Jesus the most often, and he got himself in trouble more than anyone else. When Simon Peter was acting like the solid rock leader of the disciples, Jesus called him Peter, but when he was wishy-washy and full of doubt, Jesus called him Simon.

Now, Jesus and the disciples often stayed in Peter's house in Capernaum, where he lived with his wife and his brother, Andrew. Once, Peter's mother-in-law fell terribly ill with a high fever. When Jesus took her hand and helped her up, she was instantly well, and she began to serve Jesus and his friends.

Another time, as the disciples rowed through stormy weather late at night across the Sea of Galilee, a figure walked right past the boat on the waves. It was terrifying! "Take heart; it is I. Do not be afraid" (Matthew 14:27), came Jesus' voice. Peter yelled, "Lord, call me to you on the water!" When Jesus said, "Come," Peter threw himself over the side of the boat and walked on the water toward Jesus. Once Peter looked around at the waves and wind, he began to sink into the sea, and he begged Jesus to save him. Jesus asked Peter why he doubted. Once Jesus and Peter were in the boat, the storm stopped, and the boat was suddenly at the shore. "You are the Son of God," the amazed disciples said as they worshiped Jesus.

Peter was one of Jesus' closest friends, so he saw some truly amazing sights. For instance, Peter saw Jesus transformed, with dazzling white clothes, talking to Moses and Elijah. Later, Peter was invited to pray near Jesus in the Garden of Gethsemane, before Jesus was taken to be crucified.

Sometimes, Peter's doubt overwhelmed him. When Jesus stood trial, Peter waited in the courtyard. Three times, Peter denied knowing Jesus, to protect himself from an angry crowd. When a rooster crowed at the break of dawn, Peter wept.

Peter was always too loud, too brash, and acted without thinking enough about what he was going to do. Yet, Jesus used bold, enthusiastic Peter to build his church. After Jesus was crucified, resurrected, and then raised into heaven, Peter and the disciples gathered on the day of Pentecost. Jesus sent God the Holy Spirit to fill the believers, and they all began speaking in different languages so visitors to Jerusalem understood them. Peter, full of the Holy Spirit, stood and preached. He told the people that God had promised to send the Holy Spirit to his church. God had promised, too, to send Jesus, the Messiah, to save people from their sins on the Cross and to raise him from the dead. That day, around three thousand people were saved.

Peter and John often traveled together as the church grew. Peter's wife traveled with them, too. As Peter preached through the power of the Holy Spirit, thousands of people were saved, many were healed, and demons were cast out. It was an exciting time.

Once, Peter was thrown in prison for preaching about Jesus, chained between two guards. Suddenly, an angel woke Peter and led him outside. Peter ran to the house where his friends were praying for him. He knocked and knocked, but his friends didn't open the door, for they thought his escape was impossible. Without God, it would have been.

Peter's friend John Mark wrote the Gospel of Mark to share Peter's account of Jesus' ministry. Later, Peter wrote two letters encouraging believers to persevere, even in the face of suffering and persecution. In the end, both Peter and his wife were crucified because of their faith in Jesus.

ANDREW,
THE BRINGER OF PEOPLE

The Bible is the story of God's great plan for our salvation. Because God is holy, our sin separates us from him. Long before God created the earth, he knew that we would sin—rebel—against him, so Jesus planned to come to earth, to become fully man and fully human, and to take the punishment for our sin on the Cross.

God sent John the Baptist (the son of Elizabeth who was a cousin of Mary), to tell people that Jesus— the Messiah, or Christ—was coming to save us from our sins. John the Baptist lived in the wilderness, telling people to repent of—turn from—their sins. Then he promised that the Christ was on his way. Peter's brother Andrew and his friend, John the son of Zebedee, went to listen to John the Baptist preach.

One day, John and Andrew heard John the Baptist cry out, "Behold, the Lamb of God!" as Jesus walked by. John meant that Jesus takes away the sins of the world. Andrew and John had found the Christ!

So, they started following Jesus, who invited them to come along with him. Andrew rushed to bring his brother, Peter, to Jesus. "Simon! We have found the Christ." Later, Jesus called Peter, Andrew, James, and John to become fishers of men. That's just what Andrew was—a fisher of men—for, Andrew continued to bring people to Jesus.

Later, Jesus heard that Herod Antipas the Tetrarch—the son of the King Herod who sent the

wise men to see baby Jesus—had killed John the Baptist for calling him to repent. Jesus sailed off with the disciples so they could be alone to grieve. But, a crowd of five thousand men—with women and children, too—ran ahead of the boat so they could arrive on shore before Jesus arrived.

By evening, the crowd was hungry and Jesus declared that his friends should feed them. Andrew—the bringer of people—brought to Jesus a little boy who had a picnic lunch packed with five loaves of bread and two cooked fish. "What good are these for so many people?" Andrew asked Jesus. But Jesus thanked God for the food, as he always did. Then, he broke the loaves into pieces. The disciples handed out enough food for thousands of people, and then gathered twelve baskets of leftover food.

Later, Andrew the bringer brought people to Jesus again. After Jesus entered Jerusalem on a donkey, some Greek men wanted to see Jesus. Jesus' disciple, Philip, told Andrew. Andrew brought Philip to Jesus and, together, they told their Savior about the Greek men seeking him.

Then, Jesus spoke to Philip and Andrew about his coming crucifixion. "The hour has come for the Son of

Man to be glorified. Truly, truly, I say to you, unless a grain of wheat falls into the earth and dies, it remains alone; but if it dies, it bears much fruit. Whoever loves his life loses it, and whoever hates his life in this world will keep it for eternal life. If anyone serves me, he must follow me; and where I am, there will my servant be also. If anyone serves me, the Father will honor him" (John 12:23-26).

You see, by dying, Jesus was going to take the punishment for the sins of all who believed in him.

Jesus would "bear much fruit" because we Christians are like a harvest of fruit for the kingdom of God. He was telling Philip and Andrew, too, that to serve Jesus we must love Jesus more than we love comfort, food, entertainment, books, or sports. We should love Jesus so much that all the things we enjoy seem hated by comparison.

Andrew loved Jesus that much. After Jesus was crucified, Andrew was with the other disciples when

Jesus greeted them, risen from the dead. Then, Andrew watched Jesus rise into heaven. Later, Andrew went north to bring the people of Greece, Romania, Ukraine, and southern Russia to Jesus through the gospel. Andrew was crucified, like Jesus—and like his brother Peter—for sharing the good news of salvation with others. In the end, his life bore much fruit for the kingdom of God.

JAMES,
THE SON OF THUNDER

James and his brother John were from a successful family from Galilee. Their parents were Zebedee and his wife Salome. Salome became one of the women who traveled with Jesus, providing money for Jesus' ministry, preparing meals, and caring for his many followers. James the Younger's mother was there, too.

Because there were two disciples named James, the son of Zebedee is sometimes called James the Elder. Jesus, though, called James and John "the Sons of Thunder." That's just what James and John were—they were thunderous. The brothers had fiery tempers, they were selfish, and they wanted things their way. Once, they even asked Jesus if they could call down fire on a town full of people.

Still, James was one of Jesus' closest friends. He was invited to see things only Peter and John got to experience. Once, as Jesus arrived on the shore of the Sea of Galilee, an important man named Jairus threw himself at Jesus' feet. "Come heal my daughter," he cried. "She is about to die." When Jesus, the disciples,

and a great crowd of people reached Jairus' home, there were flute players fluting and wailers wailing. "Your daughter is dead, don't bother the Teacher," said someone. Jesus turned to the crowd and said, "Do not weep, for she is not dead but sleeping" (Luke 8:52). The crowd laughed at Jesus. So, he took James, John, and Peter, along with Jairus and his wife, into the house. Then, he held the little girl's hand and said, "Child, arise." The little girl rose from the dead, and Jesus told her parents to feed her.

Another day, Jesus asked the disciples who they believed him to be. "The Christ of God," said James' friend, Peter. That was the right answer. Jesus told the disciples that to follow him meant denying themselves

and taking up their cross daily to follow him. We must not be ashamed of Jesus, or he will be ashamed of us. "But I tell you truly, there are some standing here who will not taste death until they see the kingdom of God" (Luke 9:27), Jesus said.

What did Jesus mean? Well, a week later, Jesus took James, John, and Peter to pray on the mountain. James noticed that Jesus' face looked different and his clothing was brilliantly white. Jesus was talking to Moses and Elijah from the Old Testament. James had been terribly sleepy, but now he was wide awake. He

heard Peter offer to make tents for Jesus, Moses, and Elijah. Then, a cloud covered the men and James heard the voice of God say, "This is my Son, my Chosen One; listen to him!" (Luke 9:35). In that moment, James saw a glimpse of the kingdom of God. Jesus is the King of the kingdom of God, which includes all the people from all the nations throughout all of history who have ever followed him.

Now, to take his cross daily and to follow Jesus meant James would need to humble himself. But, more than ever, James and his brother John wanted to be important in the kingdom of God. So, the Sons of Thunder became thunderous. Their mother, Salome, brought her sons and knelt before Jesus. "Say my sons will sit at your right and left hand in your kingdom," she told Jesus.

Jesus told Salome she didn't know what she was asking. "Are you able to drink the cup that I am to drink?" (Matthew 20:22b), he asked James and John. "We are able," they said confidently. But, Jesus told them, disciples of Jesus are servants of one another, even "as the Son of Man came not to be served but to serve, and to give his life as a ransom for many" (Matthew 10:28).

Jesus was talking to James and John about the cup of God's wrath. Jesus was going to take the punishment for the sins of all his followers on the Cross. Now, James was saved by Jesus Christ and his sins were forgiven, avoiding God's wrath. He did, however, suffer as he followed Jesus. After Jesus' Resurrection, James was an important elder in the church in Jerusalem until Herod Antipas had James killed with the sword.

THE WOMEN WHO FOLLOWED JESUS

God's Word tells us many women followed Jesus, serving Jesus' ministry. Some of the women were mothers of the disciples, and some were healed of demons or illnesses by Jesus. We know little about most of the women, but the Bible names Susanna and Joanna, who was the wife of Chuza, the manager of Herod of Galilee's household. James and John, the Sons of Thunder, brought their mother, Salome, with them.

Two women named Mary traveled with Jesus as he taught. Mary Magdalene was the sister of Martha and Lazarus, who Jesus raised from the dead. The mother of the disciple James the Younger and his brother Joses also traveled with Jesus. Jesus' mother was named Mary, and she joined the disciples at the cross.

JOHN,
THE BELOVED DISCIPLE

Like his brother James, John was a Son of Thunder. As the time drew closer to Jesus' crucifixion, he traveled from Galilee toward Jerusalem in Judea. Jesus sent messengers into a village in Samaria, asking them to prepare for his arrival. Jews and Samaritans did not get along, so the villagers refused to serve Jesus. In their fiery, entitled way, the Sons of Thunder asked Jesus, "Lord, do you want us to call down fire from

heaven to burn them up?" Whoa. Jesus turned and rebuked them.

Another time, the disciples were arguing over who was the greatest. Jesus asked what they were discussing. When no one would answer, Jesus showed them a child from the crowd. "If anyone would be first, he must be last of all and servant of all... Whoever receives one such child in my name receives me, and whoever receives me, receives not me but him who sent me" (Mark 9:35, 37). You see when we serve Jesus humbly, we can't be worried over who is the greatest. The greatest is always Jesus.

After the Last Supper in the upper room, Jesus took the disciples to the Garden of Gethsemane to pray. He took John, James, and Peter with him to pray apart from the group. Then, Jesus prayed alone, a little further away. Jesus knew he would be dying on the cross, so, he asked God to remove his cup of wrath from him. Then, he promised to do the Father's will, no matter what. Three times Jesus prayed, and three times his friends slept while they were supposed to be praying. Finally, the chief priests, scribes, and elders arrived with soldiers to arrest Jesus.

John knew the high priest who arrested Jesus, so he was allowed to enter the high priest's courtyard while Peter stood at the door. John followed Jesus to the cross, too. He and his mother, Salome, and the other women stood with Jesus' mother Mary as Jesus hung on the cross. Jesus looked down and said to Mary, "Woman, behold, your son!" To John, he said, "Behold, your mother" (John 19:26-27). From that day, John cared for Mary, Jesus' mother.

Jesus was buried on a Friday afternoon. On Sunday morning, Mary Magdalene told John and Peter that Jesus was not in the tomb. John outran Peter, and looking into the tomb he saw the linen cloths Jesus' body had been wrapped in lying there. The cloth that had covered his face was folded beside them. Jesus was alive!

After his Resurrection, Jesus appeared to the disciples, to the women, and even to five hundred believers at one time. Jesus remained on earth for forty days, preparing the disciples. At one point, Jesus told Peter he would be crucified. Peter pointed to John, saying, "Well, what about this man, Lord?" Jesus said, "If it is my will that he remain until I come, what is that to you? You follow me!" (John 21:22).

After Jesus' Resurrection, John and Peter traveled together, making disciples and performing signs and wonders through the Holy Spirit. Many, many people came to faith in Jesus. In fact, John's disciples became fathers of the early church. Polycarp became the bishop of the church in Smyrna, Turkey. Ignatius became the head of the church in Antioch in Syria.

John, of course, did die—of old age. In fact, he was the only disciple not killed for being a follower of Jesus. That doesn't mean things weren't hard for him. He must have grieved when his brother James was killed. Jesus had explained that the world—unbelievers—hate God and hate Jesus, so the world hates followers of Jesus, too. John wrote about that in his Gospel—the story of Jesus' ministry, in John 15:18-25.

John wrote his Gospel and three letters to the church. The formerly fiery Son of Thunder became so humble that he didn't even write his own name—instead, he wrote "the disciple whom Jesus loved." When John was banished to the island of Patmos off the coast of Greece, God gave him a vision of his plan for history and salvation. John saw, too, the new heaven and new earth that Jesus will bring when he returns for his people. John wrote it all down in the book of Revelation.

PHILIP,
THE SLOW OF HEART

The day after Andrew, John, and Peter met Jesus in the wilderness, they traveled together to Galilee. Walking past Philip, Jesus simply said, "Follow me." When Jesus moves someone's heart to follow him, they always do. In fact, in John 15:16, Jesus tells the disciples, "You did not choose me, but I chose you and appointed you." That's how it is for each of Jesus' followers.

Right away, Philip sought out his friend Nathanael, saying, "We found the one Moses wrote about in the Law, and the prophets wrote about. He is Jesus of Nazareth, the son of Joseph." Nathanael was skeptical, so Philip just said, "Come and see!" When Nathanael met God the Son face-to-face, he, too, became a disciple.

Philip was not fiery like the Sons of Thunder or bold like Peter. Philip was a just-the-facts-please guy, the kind of man who got possible-to-do things done. Philip was there when the five thousand hungry men—with their wives and children—followed Jesus to the mountain. Before Andrew brought the little boy and his lunch to Jesus, Jesus asked Philip, "Where are we to buy bread, so that these people may eat?" (John 6:5). Now, Jesus was testing Philip, who objected, "Two hundred denarii worth of bread would not be enough for each of them to get a little food." That's like saying, "Jesus, one man could work six days a week for more than eight months, and we still wouldn't have enough money to feed everyone." Jesus showed Philip he could feed everyone anyway.

The night before his crucifixion, Jesus said, "I am the way, and the truth, and the life. No one comes to the

Father except through me. If you had known me, you would have known my Father also. From now on you do know him and have seen him" (John 14:6-7).

You and I know that our one, true God is three Persons in one God—God the Father, God the Son, and God the Holy Spirit. Jesus told his disciples that speaking to God the Son is the same as speaking to God the Father—they are one God. But Philip, after three years of miracles, signs, and teaching from Jesus, said, "Lord, show us the Father, and it is enough for us" (John 14:8).

Jesus replied, "Have I been with you so long, and you still do not know me, Philip? Whoever has seen me has seen the Father. How can you say, "Show us the Father'? Do you not believe that I am in the Father and the Father is in me? The words that I say to you I do not speak on my own authority, but the Father who dwells in me does his works" (John 14:9-10).

Philip, our just-the-facts guy, had completely missed the facts that were right in front of him. He was slow of heart, as Jesus sometimes called the disciples. Philip's life was changed completely when he

saw Jesus rise from the dead and ascend to heaven. It was a fact Philip couldn't miss.

After Judas Iscariot died, the apostles prayed and chose Matthias to become the twelfth apostle. The church was multiplying as thousands of new people became followers of Jesus, and with all the new believers, there were new needs, especially among the women who had been widowed, for their husbands had died and they needed someone to care for them. Christians care for each other with the love of Jesus, but gathering and distributing food was just too much for the apostles to do on top of preaching and praying.

So, the apostles chose seven wise, godly men as deacons, including Stephen and another man named Philip. The stories in the book of Acts are all about the new deacon Philip, not Jesus' disciple Philip.

The apostle Philip became a fisher of men in places like Greece, Syria, and Turkey, bringing many people to Jesus as they heard the gospel through his preaching. Just eight years after James died for his faith, Philip was martyred, too. Today, he is with Jesus in heaven. One day, all believers will live together with Jesus.

NATHANIEL
BARTHOLOMEW, THE TRUE OF HEART

Jesus was born in Bethlehem, Judea, where King David was born a little over a thousand years before. After the birth, Jesus, his mother Mary, and Mary's husband Joseph fled to Egypt when an angel directed Joseph to protect little Jesus. Later, Joseph moved his family back to his hometown, Nazareth. This was right where two busy roads leading around the Mediterranean Sea intersected.

Nathanael Bartholomew was born in Cana, a small town in Galilee. His last name Bartholomew, or Bar-Tolmai, means the son of Tolmai. Cana was a little town that people really had to want to visit since it wasn't on a main road.

Both Nazareth and Cana were in the northern region of Galilee, where men worked with their hands. Jesus was a carpenter. The disciples Peter, James, and John, and perhaps Nathanael, Philip, and Thomas as well, were fishermen. Jewish boys in Galilee attended school at their local synagogue and memorized the Old Testament Scriptures. Still, the people of Galilee had the reputation of being uneducated.

Nathanael, though, loved God's Word. Like his friend Philip, he was excited about the coming of the Christ—the Messiah, and he was anxious to find out who would fulfill God's prophecies in the Old Testament. Even so, when Philip said to Nathanael, "We found the one Moses wrote about in the Law, and the prophets wrote about. He is Jesus of Nazareth, the son of Joseph," Nathanael didn't jump up in excitement. Instead, he asked, "Can anything good come out of Nazareth?" Philip just said, "Come and see." So, Nathanael did.

When Jesus saw Nathanael coming, he said, "Behold, an Israelite indeed, in whom there is no deceit!" (John 1:47). Jesus knew Nathanael was a sincere student of the Word of God, and that he loved the Lord. However, Nathaniel didn't know why Jesus would talk about his heart being true—faithful and without deceit. "How do you know me?" he asked.

Jesus answered Nathanael, "Before Philip called you, when you were under the fig tree, I saw you" (John 1:48). No one but God can see us wherever we are, and only God truly knows our heart, so Nathanael cried out, "Rabbi," which means Teacher, "You are the Son of God! You are the King of Israel!" Then, Jesus told Nathanael

that he would see much greater things than what Jesus had just shown him.

Three days later, Nathanael attended a wedding with Jesus, the disciples, and Jesus' mother, Mary, in Nathanael's hometown, Cana, about a three-hour walk from Nazareth. Mary knew that Jesus is the Son of God, born to her under miraculous circumstances. So, when the wine at the wedding ran out, she said to Jesus, "They have no wine." Jesus replied, "Woman, what does this have to do with me? My hour has not yet come" (John 2:4). Jesus meant he was not yet ready to save people by dying on the Cross. He wasn't ready to tell the world he is the Christ, either.

Mary knew Jesus would help her, so she turned to the servants at the wedding, and said, "Do whatever Jesus tells you." Jesus had the servants fill six stone jars, each with twenty or thirty gallons of water. Then, he told them to take a cupful of liquid from one of the jars and bring it to the master of the feast. The master of the feast declared the water-turned-wine to be the best served. This was Jesus' first miracle. It was a sign that showed that he is the Christ, the Son of God. Nathanael and his friends were amazed, and they believed in Jesus.

Nathanael spent three years learning from Jesus. Early Church historians, like Eusebius and Jerome, reported that—after the Resurrection of Jesus—Nathanael traveled to India to share the gospel. But, the names and borders of countries change over time, and they may have meant today's countries of Ethiopia or Yemen. We know Nathanael and Judas (not Iscariot) went together to Armenia to preach. Nathanael was martyred for his faith in Jesus, but we are not sure how or where he died.

MATTHEW LEVI,
THE TAX COLLECTOR

Matthew, the son of Alphaeus from Capernaum, had a Jewish name—Levi. Matthew Levi knew the Old Testament well. Even so, when Jesus walked past Matthew and said, "Follow me," his disciples must have been shocked.

You see, Matthew wasn't a fisherman, a carpenter, or even a merchant. Matthew was a tax collector. The Roman Empire required the people of each territory they conquered to obey the Roman emperor and

the regional kings. Rome also forced people to pay taxes through Jewish tax collectors. The tax collectors took the people's money and sent it to Rome. First, though, they added money to the tax bill and kept it for themselves—it was stealing.

Tax collectors taxed everything. So, if your donkey pulled a cart full of fish past the tax booth, the tax collector might collect taxes on your donkey, on the wheels of your wagon, on your fish, and then add a tax for using the road. He may even charge you a tax he made up that very day. As you might imagine, tax collectors were not popular. People hated them. Tax collectors weren't even allowed to enter the synagogue to worship God.

Now, when Jesus told Matthew to follow him, Matthew did. He just left his booth and ran after Jesus. Matthew was so excited about following Jesus that he invited all his friends to a big feast at his house. Now, Matthew's friends were also tax collectors, thieves, and committed sinners. They were the worst of the worst. When the Jewish religious leaders—the scribes and Pharisees—saw Jesus and his friends at a huge banquet for tax collectors, they wrinkled their noses and pursed their lips. "Why does your teacher eat with tax collectors and sinners?" they asked the disciples. Jesus replied, "Those who are well have no need of a physician, but those who are sick. Go and learn what this means: 'I desire mercy, and not sacrifice.' For I came not to call the righteous, but sinners" (Matthew 9:12-13).

You see, Jesus heals us from our sins. But, he doesn't heal people who refuse to recognize their sins. We are saved if we believe in Jesus, confess our belief with our

mouths, and turn away from our sins to follow Jesus. The Pharisees made a terrible mistake when they assumed that Matthew's sin was worse than theirs. Just one sin separates us from God, and God's Word tells us that "all have sinned and fall short of the glory of God" (Romans 3:23). Jesus is the only innocent person who ever lived.

During his ministry, Jesus often told stories with hidden meanings, called parables. Matthew must have heard many parables, several of which were about treasure. After Jesus was crucified and raised from the dead, he rose to heaven. Matthew then wrote the Gospel of Matthew about Jesus' ministry.

In Matthew 13:44, he recorded this story that Jesus told: "The kingdom of heaven is like treasure hidden in a field, which a man found and covered up. Then in

his joy, he goes and sells all that he has and buys that field." Following Jesus is worth so much, we should be excited to give up everything else if he asks us to do so, just like Matthew did when he left behind his riches to serve Jesus.

Matthew wrote his Gospel for the Jewish people, who knew the Old Testament well. Matthew knew Scripture well, too. In fact, he quotes the Old Testament ninety-nine times in his book, showing how Jesus fulfilled the prophecies God gave his people.

Matthew stayed in Judea to preach the good news to Jews before visiting the people of Iran and Ethiopia. Like his fellow disciples-turned-apostles, Matthew was killed because he loved and preached about Jesus. In his revelation to John, Jesus tells his followers, "Be faithful unto death, and I will give you the crown of life" (Revelation 2:10). In our forever home with Jesus, there will be a special crown—a reward—given to those who are martyred for their faith in Christ.

THOMAS,
THE TWIN

After Jesus had called the first seven disciples, he prayed all night to his Father God in the Holy Spirit on the mountain. The next morning, he called Thomas, another James, Simon the Zealot, and two men named Judas—one who would betray him and one who would not. Jesus called them to follow him. Jesus' twelve disciples were his closest group of friends.

The Jewish religious leaders—the scribes, Pharisees, and Sadducees—loved power, and they had lots of it. Jesus claimed to be the Son of God—the Christ, our Savior—and God the Son—the second Person of our Triune God, who has always existed. They didn't like that at all. So, they plotted to kill Jesus. Because of all the people following him, they waited for a time when they could find Jesus alone. But Jesus and his disciples were not staying in Jerusalem—the home of the temple and the chief priests.

However, something happened that took Jesus back to that area. Jesus' friend, Lazarus, suddenly became ill. Lazarus lived in Bethany, just six miles from Jerusalem. His sisters, Mary Magdalene and Martha, sent someone to tell Jesus. After two days, Jesus announced they were going to see Lazarus. "Wait!" said his disciples. "Why would we travel anywhere near the Jews who want to stone you?" Jesus replied, "Our friend Lazarus has fallen asleep, but I go to awaken him" (John 11:11). The disciples thought Lazarus was resting, so Jesus told them, "Lazarus has died, and for your sake, I am glad that I was not there, so that you may believe. But let us go to him" (John 11:14).

Now, Thomas—born a twin—was a practical man. He wanted to make the best decisions he could with all the information available. Thomas realized that the Jewish leaders really wanted to kill Jesus. Also, Lazarus was really dead, and Jesus could really raise Lazarus to life. Jesus was going to Bethany where danger waited for him, and if Jesus was going to die, Thomas was ready to die, too. So, he said to his friends, "Let's all go, so that we can all die with Jesus."

Lazarus' body had been rotting for four days in the tomb when Martha ran to ask Jesus to raise him to life. Jesus replied, "I am the resurrection and the

life. Whoever believes in me, though he die, yet shall he live, and everyone who lives and believes in me shall never die. Do you believe this?" (John 11:25-26). Martha confessed, "I believe you are the Christ, the Son of God!" Jesus cried with Mary and the crowd because he loved Lazarus. Then Jesus thanked his Father for always hearing him. Finally, Jesus called in a loud voice, "Lazarus, come out," so Lazarus did.

Later, Jesus went up to Jerusalem for the Passover feast. In the upper room, he told the disciples, "In my Father's house are many rooms. If it were not so, would I have told you that I go to prepare a place for

you? And if I go and prepare a place for you, I will come again and will take you to myself, that where I am you may be also. And you know the way to where I am going" (John 14:2-4).

Wait a minute! Thomas needed all the information. "Lord," he objected. "We do not know where you are going. How will we know the way?" After all, Thomas did not want to get left behind. Jesus responded, "I am the way, and the truth, and the life. No one comes to the Father except through me" (John 14:6). You see, Jesus is the only way to the Father. If we know

and follow Jesus, he will make sure we get to the place he has prepared for us.

When Jesus rose from the dead, he appeared to Thomas, showing him the scars from his wounds on the Cross. Thomas cried out, "My Lord and my God!" Thomas believed in Jesus as his Lord and his God for the rest of his life. He traveled to Iran and then to India setting up churches. Believers today say that Thomas traveled into China, sharing the good news of Jesus, before returning to his work in India. Many, many people became believers in Jesus before Thomas was killed with a spear.

JAMES,
THE YOUNGER

James was the son of Alphaeus—or Clopas—and Mary. Mary also followed Jesus, possibly with James' brother—called Joses or Joseph. Now, James was a popular name in the time of Jesus, just as it is today. James the son of Alphaeus is sometimes confused for John's brother James—the Son of Thunder (sometimes

called James the Elder), or for Jesus' brother James—the author of the book of the Bible titled *James*. Because of that, the Bible refers to the disciple James as James the Younger or James the Less.

Jesus' twelve disciples traveled with him for a while as his closest friends and students. Then, Jesus gave them the power and authority to cast out demons and to cure diseases. These signs and wonders showed that Jesus truly is the Christ.

Do you ever wonder what a demon is? Well, in the beginning, God made the heavens and the earth and everything in between. He also made spiritual creatures, called angels, to serve him. Satan, who was a created angel, rebelled against God in his pride, leading a third of the angels to disobey God. So, God threw them out of heaven. These angels are now demons—evil spirits who try to hurt their Creator God by harming and misleading his people here on earth. It is important to remember that Jesus—as God the Son—is the Creator of all things. He made the demons, so in the Gospels, demons will sometimes state that they know him because they were once in heaven serving him. Christians don't need to be afraid of demons, because our King Jesus has all power and authority over them.

So, Jesus sent James and the rest of the disciples to preach, without taking food, money, or extra clothing. They also wouldn't receive payment—they were there to announce that the Christ—the Son of God—has come to forgive sins! Instead, they depended on God's provision for them through his people. James and his friends traveled from town to town through Galilee and Judea in groups of two, telling people, "The kingdom of heaven is here. Repent and turn from your sin. Follow Jesus!" Then, they cast demons out of people, healed terrible illnesses, restored the skin of lepers, and removed disabilities. James and his friends even raised people from the dead.

It must have been a sad day for James when Jesus was arrested in the Garden of Gethsemane while he was with his disciples. James knew Jesus was innocent. The reason Jesus was able to take our punishment on the cross is that he never sinned—he is, after all, fully God and fully man, God the Son and the Son of God.

After Jesus was tried, mocked, and beaten, he was made to carry his cross to the Place of the Skull, Golgotha. The Romans would crucify him there. People mocked Jesus while his wrists and feet were nailed to the wood. In his Gospel, Luke tells us that all Jesus' acquaintances were there at a distance, so we can assume James came to watch with his mother

Mary, Salome—James and John's mother, Mary Magdalene, and the other women as Jesus took the punishment for our sins.

After Jesus died, a man named Joseph from the town of Arimathea took Jesus' body to be buried in Joseph's own newly cut tomb. Mary—James' mother, and the other women followed Joseph and saw where Jesus' body was laid on Friday evening. On Sunday morning, James' mother Mary went with Mary Magdalene and the other women to the tomb. They found the tomb empty with the stone rolled away and two angels told

them that Jesus had risen from the dead. Mary ran to tell her son James and the other disciples that Jesus is alive.

After Jesus ascended to heaven, the disciples went out to share the good news of Jesus just as they had done when he sent them out two by two during his ministry. James traveled to preach, possibly in Syria and Iran, and was martyred for his teaching that Jesus is the Christ. James knew without any doubt that Jesus died for our sins and rose again—he saw it with his own eyes.

JUDAS
LEBBAEUS THADDAEUS, NOT ISCARIOT

Just as there were two disciples named Simon and two disciples named James, there were also two disciples named Judas. Only one of the men named Judas betrayed Jesus. Perhaps for this reason, the authors of the Gospels called the faithful Judas by several names. He was called Lebbaeus with the last name Thaddaeus,

or by his last name alone, or Judas the son of James, or Judas (not Iscariot). Judas Lebbaeus Thaddaeus was not Judas Iscariot, nor was he Jude, the brother of Jesus, who wrote a very short book of the New Testament.

At the end of Jesus' ministry during the Passover feast, the disciples gathered in the upper room. Now, Jesus knew that Satan had already whispered into the heart of Judas Iscariot—the other Judas. Judas (not Iscariot) and the disciples sat around the table, unconcerned. Had they known Jesus was going to be arrested, tried, and nailed to a cross in just a few hours, perhaps they would have acted differently. But they were not worried.

During the New Testament, men wore sandals and walked on dirt roads, so their feet were always covered in dust and muck. It was customary for a servant to bring a bowl of water so they could wash their dirty feet before they ate. There was no servant to help the disciples, so Jesus tied a towel around his waist, poured water into a bowl, and began to wash the dirty feet of his disciples. Then, Jesus dried their clean feet with the towel around his waist. "Do you understand what I have done to you?" he asked the disciples. "You call me Teacher and Lord, and you are right, for so I am. If I then, your Lord and Teacher, have washed your feet, you also ought to wash one another's feet."

Judas and the others were probably uncomfortable. They should have served Jesus. Instead, they waited for someone else to serve them. Jesus continued, "For I have given you an example, that you also should do just as I have done to you. Truly, truly, I say to you, a servant is not greater than his master, nor is a messenger greater than the one who sent him" (John 13:12-16).

At dinner, Jesus told Peter he would deny Jesus—and Peter strongly disagreed. Jesus said he was going to prepare a place for the disciples so that they could all be together—but Thomas was worried that they wouldn't be able to find this place. "Lord, we don't know where you are going, so how can we know the way?" Jesus told him that he is the way, the truth, and the life, and the only way to the Father is through him. This was when Philip said that he wanted to see the Father.

Next, Jesus told the disciples that God the Father would send God the Holy Spirit to dwell in the disciples. He said the world could not receive the Holy Spirit. Then, Jesus said that anyone who keeps his commandments loves him. And, if they love Jesus, the Father will love them, and Jesus will love them, and Jesus will show himself to them.

Now, maybe Judas (not Iscariot) was hoping that Jesus would make himself the king of this world and show himself to everyone. Jesus, though, is the King

of the Universe—he always has been. Still, Judas (not Iscariot) asked, "Lord, how will you show yourself to us, and not to the world?" Judas wanted to know why everyone wouldn't know about Jesus being King, all at once.

Jesus answered him, "If anyone loves me, he will keep my word, and my Father will love him, and we will come to him and make our home with him" (John 14:23). You see, God the Holy Spirit lives in the hearts

of believers. We know Jesus is King. One day, Jesus will show himself to all the world when he returns for his people.

After Jesus was crucified and rose again, he ascended to heaven. The Holy Spirit did come to live in the hearts of believers on the day of Pentecost. Peter preached, and around three thousand people were saved. Judas was there to see all of it. Later, full of the Holy Spirit, Judas went north with Nathanael to preach the good news of Jesus in Armenia, Syria, Libya, and Turkey. Eventually, the people who hated Jesus killed Judas, perhaps with a club or an axe. Judas, though, earned the crown of life.

SIMON,
THE ZEALOT

When a person believes in Jesus, confesses their belief with their mouth, and repents of their sin, they are saved. Then, the Holy Spirit lives in their heart, and they become more and more like Jesus. For instance, Peter was bold and brash—and he became a powerful gospel preacher. John was thunderous and fiery—and he became known as the apostle of love. How do we

know Simon was changed when he is only listed in the Bible as one of the disciples? Well, Matthew, Mark, and Luke call him Simon the Zealot—and the word Zealot means something.

After Moses, God gave the Jewish people the Promised Land as their inheritance from God. When they continued to disobey God—following false gods, worshiping God in false ways, and showing false justice to their neighbors, God exiled them from the land. He kicked them out. Years later, God allowed the Jewish people to return to Israel, but it wasn't the same. By the time of Jesus, the Roman Empire ruled over the land that was once the kingdom of David.

When Jesus was around ten or twelve years old, a man named Judas the Galilean led a violent revolt against Rome. Judas was killed, but his men—Zealots—continued to believe that only God could rule the Jewish people and that taxes were treason against God. They believed God was sending a Messiah, but they wanted him to be a military leader. Because the Zealots didn't have a large army, they attacked and burned buildings, stabbing Roman officials, soldiers, and even tax collectors before running into the crowd to hide.

We know that Simon was a Zealot. He was a terrorist committed to taking Israel back by force. It must have

been a surprise to Simon when he was saved by Jesus and he became a brother in Christ to Matthew, the former tax collector.

Maybe Simon felt a surge of excitement when, after three years with Jesus, and after Jesus' triumphal entry into Jerusalem on a donkey, Jesus cleansed the temple. When Jesus entered the temple—where the Jewish people were supposed to worship God rightly by God's rules—he saw his house being treated like a marketplace. There were people exchanging money as in a bank and men selling pigeons to be sacrificed. Jesus turned over all the tables and the chairs and drove out

the merchants saying, "It is written, 'My house shall be called a house of prayer,' but you make it a den of robbers" (Matthew 21:13).

Simon was probably surprised, though, by Jesus' answer when Pharisees tried to trick him. "Hey, Teacher," the Pharisees said, feeling very sneaky indeed. "We know you don't care about anyone else's opinion, so tell us if it's lawful to pay taxes to Caesar—the emperor." If Jesus answered yes, he might get stabbed in the back by a Zealot. If he answered no, he might find himself in trouble with the emperor. But, God is in charge of all governments, emperors, and

even taxes. So, Jesus asked the Pharisees why they would test him. Jesus asked them whose face was on a Roman coin. "It is Caesar's," they said. Jesus answered them, Give "to Caesar the things that are Caesar's, and to God the things that are God's" (Mark 12:17). The Pharisees—and probably Simon, too—were amazed at Jesus' wise answer.

About forty years after Jesus died and rose again, the Zealots rebelled in Jerusalem. The future emperor, Titus Vespasian, came to end the rebellion. But, the Zealots refused to surrender, even killing fellow Jews who wanted to end the fighting. In the end, the Roman army destroyed Jerusalem. Thousands of Jews died and the temple was stripped of anything valuable. All the warring of the Zealots came to death, destruction, and despair.

Simon the Zealot's life, though, changed when he became a disciple of Jesus. No longer a terrorist, Simon became an apostle of God. After the fall of Jerusalem, Simon traveled to Egypt, North Africa, Iran, and perhaps north to the British Isles, sharing the good news of Jesus along the way until he was killed for his faith. One day believers in him will spend eternity with Jesus, just like Simon the no-longer-Zealot is doing today.

JUDAS
ISCARIOT, THE BETRAYER

The word disciple means to be a follower—someone who learns from a teacher. Judas Iscariot was anything but a follower. Instead, Judas Iscariot was an imposter, a traitor, and a betrayer. Iscariot probably means "man of Kerioth." Maybe Judas was from the town of Kerioth-hezron in the southern part of the region of Judea. While the other disciples all grew up in Galilee, Judas was an outsider. Still, they treated him as a

brother in Christ. For three years, he traveled, slept, ate, and laughed with the disciples, yet they never once suspected that he did not love Jesus.

Now, Jesus knew Judas Iscariot was his betrayer. For, Jesus created Judas. Jesus planned history. Remember, too, that before Jesus called the twelve disciples to become his closest friends, he prayed all night long to his Father God through God the Holy Spirit. It was not a mistake or a surprise that Judas Iscariot became a disciple, just as it was not a surprise that Jesus was crucified. All of it was a part of God's great plan for salvation.

After raising Lazarus from the dead and before going to Jerusalem for the Passover, Jesus attended a feast thrown by Lazarus and his friends. Martha was serving dinner when Mary brought an alabaster stone jar full of expensive ointment from India. Pouring the perfume all over Jesus' feet, Mary wiped his feet with her hair.

Judas was furious—because of his selfishness and greed. You see, Judas was the group treasurer, in charge of the moneybag. He loved to dip his hand into there and deposit the coins in his own pocket instead. "Why wasn't this ointment sold for a year's wages?" he scoffed. "We could have given the money to the

poor." Jesus replied, "The poor you always have with you, but you do not always have me" (John 12:8).

So, Judas—full of hate—went to the chief priests. The priests were still looking for a way to arrest Jesus in private so they could kill him. Jesus was very popular. They feared that if they arrested him while he was preaching the crowds might kill them instead. Judas asked the chief priests, "How much will you give me to deliver Jesus to you?" So, they promised Judas thirty pieces of silver.

Just six days later, in the upper room during the Last Supper, Jesus said, "Truly, I say to you, one of you will

betray me, one who is eating with me" (Mark 14:18). Like each of us, the disciples were sinners, even though they were followers of Jesus. They looked around at each other, and no one looked like a betrayer. Each of them wondered, 'Maybe it will be me.' So, around the table, one by one, they each asked, "Is it me?" Judas, too, asked, "Is it I, Rabbi?"—even though he knew the answer. Jesus said, "You have said so" (Matthew 26:25).

"What you are going to do, do quickly" (John 13:27), Jesus said to Judas. When Judas left the upper room,

none of his friends knew where he was going. They thought that perhaps he had some business activities to attend to. Judas, though, went straight to the chief priests.

When Jesus and the disciples went to the Garden of Gethsemane to pray that night, Judas led the chief priests there, along with other Pharisees, officers, and a band of soldiers. The mob was carrying lanterns, torches, and weapons. It must have been a terrifying sight. Judas walked right up to Jesus and went to kiss him on the cheek.

Simon (The Zealot)

Andrew

Thomas

Philip

Nathanael

M

Jesus was crucified for our sins and rose again. Judas, though, was wracked with guilt. Instead of repenting and turning to finally follow Jesus, Judas threw the thirty pieces of silver at the feet of the chief priests and hung himself from a tree. The Pharisees used the money to buy the field Judas died in as a place to bury unclaimed bodies. They called the place the Field of Blood. It was, after all, a place bought with money that purchased the blood of an innocent man—Jesus.

Judas (Thaddeus)

hunder)

Matthias

Peter (Simon)

James (Younger)

James (Thunder)

FOLLOW JESUS FOR ETERNAL LIFE

Jesus was teaching when a man knelt and asked him, "What do I need to do to inherit eternal life?" Jesus told him he must keep the commandments. The man asked, "Which ones?" Jesus replied, "You shall not murder, You shall not commit adultery, You shall not steal, You shall not bear false witness, Honor your father and mother, and, You shall love your neighbor as yourself" (Matthew 19:18-19).

The man breathed a sigh of relief, "I have kept all of these!" Then, Jesus told him to sell all his possessions, give the money to the poor, and follow him. Now, the young man was very rich. He was not willing to love Jesus more than his moneybags full of coins. So, he went away, sad that he would never see heaven.

Peter said to Jesus, "We left everything to follow you. What will we have?" Jesus told the disciples they would one day sit on twelve thrones, judging the twelve tribes of Israel. Then, Jesus said, "Truly, I say to you, there is no one who has left house or brothers or sisters or mother or father or children or lands, for my sake and for the gospel, who will not receive a hundredfold now in this time, houses and brothers and sisters and mothers and children and lands, with persecutions, and in the age to come eternal life. But many who are first will be last, and the last first" (Mark 10:29-31).

Anyone who loves and believes in Jesus and turns from their sin to follow him, will be with him for all eternity just as the disciples are now.

TIMELINE

c. 6/4 BC

Jesus is born in Bethlehem.

AD 6

- The Roman Empire makes Judea a Roman region.
- Judas the Galilean leads the Zealots in an uprising against Roman taxes on Jewish citizens.

c. 28-29

John the Baptist ministers near the Jordan River. Several of the disciples, looking for the Messiah, spend time following John.

c. 28-30

- Jesus begins and works his public ministry, sharing the gospel, teaching disciples, and healing the sick.
- Jesus calls the twelve disciples to follow him.

c. 30

- Jesus is crucified. He is raised from the dead and forty days later, he ascends to heaven.
- Judas Iscariot hangs himself.
- Jesus' half brother James witnesses the risen Jesus and becomes a Christian.
- Jesus sends the Holy Spirit to the believers gathered in Jerusalem and Pentecost occurs. The apostles begin to proclaim the gospel.

33/34

Jesus reveals himself to Paul on the way to Damascus and calls him to be an apostle to the nations.

36

Pilate is removed as governor due to incompetence.

37-41

Caligula is Emperor of Rome. He terrorizes his subjects.

40-45

James, the half brother of Jesus, writes a letter to Jewish believers scattered outside of Israel.

41-44

- Herod Agrippa, the grandson of Herod the Great, kills James the brother of John.
- Peter is imprisoned by Herod Agrippa.
- Herod Agrippa is killed by an angel of the Lord.

46-47

Paul goes on his first missionary journey.

48/49-51

Paul goes on his second missionary journey.

49-51

Paul writes 1 and 2 Thessalonians.

50-54

Peter comes to Rome.

51

Paul visits the church at Corinth.

52-57

Paul goes on his third missionary journey.

52-55

Paul ministers in Ephesus.

53-55

- Mark writes his Gospel, based on Peter's testimony.
- Matthew writes his Gospel.
- Paul writes 1 Corinthians while he is in Ephesus.

54-68

The reign of Roman Emperor Nero, who persecuted the church.

55-56

Paul writes 2 Corinthians while in Macedonia.

c. 55-57

Paul writes 1 Corinthians to the church at Corinth. At the time that he writes his letter, many of the 500 brothers Jesus appeared to are still alive.

57

Paul writes Romans from Corinth.

60-70

Hebrews is written by an unknown author.

62

- James, Jesus' half brother, is martyred by the Sadducee high priest, Ananas.
- Peter writes 1 Peter while in Rome.
- Paul writes Ephesians, Philippians, Colossians, Philemon, and Philemon while under arrest in Rome.
- Luke, Paul's doctor and traveling companion, writes the Gospel of Luke and Acts.

62-64

- Paul writes 1 Timothy from Macedonia.
- Paul writes Titus from Nicopolis.

64

The Roman Emperor Nero blames Christians for a massive fire in Rome and kills many believers in the first mass persecution of Christians.

64-67

- Peter writes 2 Peter.
- Jude, the half brother of Jesus, writes his letter.
- Paul writes 2 Timothy.
- Paul and Peter die for sake of the gospel in Rome.

70

The Roman army, under Emperor Titus, lays siege to Jerusalem for five months, murders the high priest Ananias, and destroys the temple.

79

Mount Vesuvius erupts and destroys Pompeii and Herculaneum.

79-81

Titus is the Emperor of Rome.

81-95

The reign of Roman Emperor Domitian, who persecutes Christians.

89-95

John, the only apostle who is not martyred, writes 1-3 John and the Gospel of John, probably while in Ephesus.

95-96

John writes Revelation while exiled to the island of Patmos by Roman Emperor Domitian.

96-98

Trajan is the Emperor of Rome.

c. 100

John dies of old age on Patmos.

Pontius Pilate becomes the governor of Judea.

WORKS CONSULTED

Currid, John D. and David P. Barrett. *Crossway ESV Bible Atlas.* Crossway, 2010.

Curtis, Ken, Ph.D. "What Happened to the 12 Disciples and Apostles of Jesus?." Christianity. https://www.christianity.com/church/church-history/timeline/1-300/whatever-happened-to-the-twelve-apostles-11629558.html. April 2, 2024. Accessed May 24, 2024.

Dodson, Rhett P. *With a Mighty Triumph!: Christ's Resurrection and Ours.* The Banner of Truth Trust, 2021.

Elwell, Walter A. and Robert W. Yarbrough. "The Middle East in the Days of Jesus." *Encountering the New Testament: A Historical and Theological Survey, Fourth Edition.* Baker Academic, 2022.

Gribetz, Judah, Edward L. Greenstein, and Regina Stein. *The Timetables of Jewish History: A Chronology of the Most Important People and Events in Jewish History.* Simon & Schuster, 1993.

Grun, Bernard. *The Timetables of History, New 3rd Rev. ed.* Simon & Schuster, 1991.

Rose Book of Bible Charts, Maps & Time Lines. Rose Publishing, 2010.

MacArthur, John. *Twelve Ordinary Men: How the Master Shaped His Disciples for Greatness, and What He Wants to Do with You.* Thomas Nelson, 2002.

Stott, John. *The Cross of Christ.* 1986. Centennial ed., InterVarsity Press, 2021.

The ESV Study Bible™, ESV® Bible. **Crossway, 2008.**

The Twelve Disciples: The Life and Ministry of Jesus' 12 Disciples. **Rose Publishing, 2004.**

Christian Focus Publications

Our mission statement
Staying Faithful

In dependence upon God we seek to impact the world through literature faithful to His infallible Word, the Bible. Our aim is to ensure that the Lord Jesus Christ is presented as the only hope to obtain forgiveness of sin, live a useful life and look forward to heaven with Him.

Our Books are published in four imprints:

◁◯✕ CHRISTIAN FOCUS

Popular works including biographies, commentaries, basic doctrine and Christian living.

◁◯✕ MENTOR

Books written at a level suitable for Bible College and seminary students, pastors, and other serious readers. The imprint includes commentaries, doctrinal studies, examination of current issues and church history.

◁◯✕ CHRISTIAN HERITAGE

Books representing some of the best material from the rich heritage of the church.

◁◯✕ CF4KIDS

Children's books for quality Bible teaching and for all age groups: Sunday school curriculum, puzzle and activity books; personal and family devotional titles, biographies and inspirational stories – because you are never too young to know Jesus!

Christian Focus Publications Ltd,
Geanies House, Fearn, Ross-shire,
IV20 1TW, Scotland, United Kingdom.
www.christianfocus.com